RANGER RICK'S BEST FRIENDS

HI, I'M RANGER RICK, the official conservation symbol for young members of the National Wildlife Federation, and leader of the Ranger Rick Nature Clubs. On behalf of all the animals in Deep Green Wood, welcome to our world of nature and wildlife.

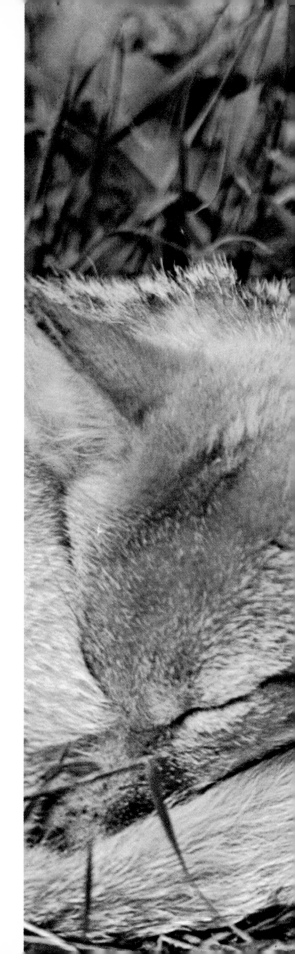

THE FOXES

by Fred Johnson

Created and Produced by
The National Wildlife Federation
Washington, D. C.

Copyright © 1973 National Wildlife Federation
Standard Book Number 912186-04-6
Library of Congress Catalog Card Number 73-83781
Second Printing, 1977

1 Reddy Fox Pays A Visit

by J. A. Brownridge

It was a beautiful, warm spring day. Ranger Rick and his friend, Roscoe Rabbit, were enjoying the sunshine as they stretched out on top of a hill just outside Deep Green Wood.

Down below them lay some fine looking farms with neat, well-painted houses and barns. In the fields, cows and horses grazed peacefully. In the barnyards, chickens strutted back and forth, pausing often to scratch the dirt, looking for food.

Farmer Jones and Mrs. Jones were working hard in their garden. The vegetables were growing very well and it looked as though they were going to have a fine crop this year.

Everything was so peaceful that, before they knew it, Rick and Roscoe had both dozed off. When they woke, it was almost dark.

"My goodness," yawned Rick. "I wonder how long we've been asleep."

"I don't know," Roscoe replied sleepily. "But I do know that I'm hungry. I think I'll just slip down and sample that nice lettuce in Farmer Jones's garden."

"You'd better not," warned Rick. "You know how angry Farmer Jones got when you and your cousins dug into his garden last week and nibbled the tops off all his new plants! The lettuce has only begun to grow back."

"Yes, doesn't it look delicious?" Roscoe asked. "But you're right, Rick. I'd better not try it again. I hopped down there yesterday, I must confess, and dug a tunnel under the big new fence Farmer Jones just built. Getting in was no problem. But right when I was in the middle of the best part of the lettuce patch —Oh! It was terrible!"

"What happened, Roscoe? Tell me!" Rick urged.

"Well, I looked up for just a moment and there was this huge dark form hurtling toward me. All I could hear was growling and all I could see was long white teeth. It was Farmer Jones's new dog!"

"I just managed to dodge him. Then I twisted away and dashed for the fence— but where was the tunnel I'd dug? As if

that wasn't bad enough, the dog's barking had brought Farmer Jones out. He had a new shotgun with him! Finally I found the hole and just ducked down into it as the dog's jaws closed behind me. I think he got some of my tail!"

"Yes, I'm afraid he did, Roscoe," Rick said, looking at what was left of the white knob. "What a horrible adventure. And you only have yourself to blame. There's plenty of good, green food out here for all of us to eat."

"That's true, Rick," Roscoe agreed. "And I'll try to stay away from Farmer Jones's, particularly now that he has the place guarded so well. But there are lots of other animals in the woods who have a hard time getting enough to eat—like Reddy Fox."

"Speak of the devil!" cried Rick. And he pointed over to the edge of the field. Coming out from the forest was a slinky, low shape, difficult to see now that the sun was down.

"Oh, oh," said Roscoe. "Reddy thinks

he's pretty smart. But he'd better look out!'' And before their eyes, Reddy slipped through Farmer Jones's barnyard and over to the henhouse.

Sniffing carefully along the walk, Reddy finally found a hole leading inside where the chickens were sleeping peacefully.

As Rick and Roscoe watched, Reddy disappeared into the henhouse. Suddenly the hens realized there was a stranger in their midst—and who the stranger was. They shrieked and flew around in a frenzy of fear.

Farmer Jones's dog, who had been locked in to protect the garden, began to growl and bark. But he could not get out and go to the hens' defense.

Farmer Jones, aroused by the racket, rushed out with his shot gun and threw open the henhouse door. Dozens of terrified chickens exploded out the door right in his face. He staggered backward and for a moment couldn't see the big red fox racing through the barnyard with a plump chicken clutched in his mouth.

But quickly the farmer recovered and found out what had happened. BLAM! BLAM! He fired both barrels of the gun he'd raised to his shoulder. But it was too late. Reddy was out of range.

''Let's follow him and see where he goes,'' suggested Rick. ''If we find his den, you'll know where to stay away from, because Reddy would like *you* just as well as that chicken.''

Cautiously, the two friends sniffed along the trail of the running fox and in a few minutes saw his den in a hillside among some rocks. Standing in the entrance were two young foxes. Reddy dropped his prize in front of them and they were soon busily engaged in having their dinner.

Off to the side Reddy stood, proud that he had had a successful hunt and his family was fed for another day.

"Isn't that a happy looking family scene?" commented Roscoe.

"It sure is," agreed Rick, "but it will cause more problems for some of our friends. When foxes leave the forest and invade barnyards, they're considered to be pests and many people want them exterminated. People often don't care about the balance of nature which calls for predators. The farmers just care about their chickens—and I might add, they care about their lettuce!"

"You mean they think I'm a predator, too?" asked Roscoe almost proudly.

"No, Roscoe, they just think of you as a pest," laughed Rick.

"The trouble is, though," he continued, "it's usually a few animals that cause that kind of trouble. Most of them avoid people as much as possible. Cleverly and silently—like Reddy Fox—they do the job nature intended them to do. Their lives and habits are very interesting, so let's read the next pages and learn all about the homes and habits of foxes."

2
Frisky Pups in the Den

When Little Red was born one bright day in April, he was just a bit larger than a hamster. He was almost helpless. His eyes were shut and he could barely crawl. He stayed close to mother and drank the nourishing warm milk she provided.

About the ninth day, Red opened his eyes. The next day he began to wobble about and explore the dim

One little fox peeks out.

His sister makes two. They wonder what's outside

world of the den his parents had prepared. Brothers and sisters bumped into each other and sniffed curiously; they all seemed to belong together. They began taking little trips across the den. Now when they were hungry they could look around and walk to find mother.

In another week Red was as big as a fat kitten. His legs were working better, and his eyes kept searching a part of his den that he hadn't reached yet. Sometimes mother disappeared in that direction. When she came back she was usually carrying something in her mouth. She would put it on the den floor and then eat it. Once she put it in front of Red. He tried a bite. It didn't taste like mother's milk, but he liked it. The

Now there are three. The bright sun makes a pup yawn.

The adult fox stretches out in the sun.
Six pups gather at the den's entrance.

other pups tried some, too, and they liked it. They had eaten their first fat insects.

One day when mother was snoozing, Red started out for the far end of the den. It was scary, but he kept going. He turned a corner and blinked his eyes.

WHAT WAS THIS? Sunlight!

Wherever he looked he saw strange, unfamiliar things. His ears turned this way and that to catch new sounds, and his little black button of a nose almost twitched itself off trying to take in all the new

10

smells. He gave an excited "Yip!" This brought all the other pups. They, too, were astonished and yipped delightedly.

At that, something that looked like mother, but bigger, came toward them from this new world. Red and the pups scrambled back to the safety of mother in the den. They had met their father.

The next day, after a long sniff and a look around, mother took the pups for

The fox catches a rabbit and *(right)* brings it home to the waiting pups.

like chase - each - other - in - zigzags, or stalk-father, or chew-on-sister's-ear-while-brother-tugs-on-your-tail. Sometimes all of them were either chewing or being chewed on, or tugging or being tugged on. Father played with them, too.

As the pups grew, mother and father showed them how to sniff out a mouse in the grass and chase it down. The mouse did not often escape the pups' zigzags. When one did go down a hole, father would dig furiously, stick his head in the hole, and come up with it. Red tried this the first time he had a chance. He came up with a mouthful of dirt, but he had the mouse.

They soon discovered other things to eat. Fruit, berries, some sweet grasses, rabbits, even young birds— all helped to fill hungry stomachs.

Red and the pups noticed that both father and mother stopped often to sniff the breeze and listen intently. So they did the same. One day they smelled and heard something new. Strange creatures' making loud frightening noises were running across the meadow. Behind them ran two different creatures on *two* legs! Man. Mother quickly sent the pups back to the den. Father ran off in another direction. The creatures

their first walk in the outside world. Father appeared and sniffed each one gently.

Red found walking outside different from walking on the hard floor of the den. He tried a small jump, and when he came down, he sort of bounced on the soft ground. The other pups tried it too, and began to run and jump about in the warm spring sun.

From then on every day was learning time. They played fine games,

12

followed him. Red and the pups never forgot that the smell and sound of men and dogs meant danger.

By the time they were six months old Red and the pups were able to go on their own hunting trips. They no longer had to depend on mother and father for food. Once Red was so far from home that he curled up in a safe spot and slept. He never went back to the den again.

He was now a young adult red fox.

3
The Young Hunter

Games are fun; the pup learns to hunt.

In the months after Red left the den where he was born, he roamed widely. Food was no problem. Red could smell and hear small creatures in the grasses. Spotting a mouse, he would crouch and leap just as if he were still a pup playing his jumping games. He seldom missed.

Rabbits became many a good meal. Red would spot a nibbling rabbit and circle cautiously up wind to begin his stalk. The rabbit would be watching for just such a danger as a creeping fox, and he would raise his head between each mouthful. When his head would go down, Red would advance, freezing instantly when it came up again. Then, when Red was close enough, and the head was down, there would be a flash of red fur through the grass. All at once, Red had his meal.

The young red fox starts out on his own. Can he catch his own food?

The red fox digs the mouse up out of the snow. The mouse tries to get away, but the fox pounces—and traps it.

Or if the rabbit twisted and turned in surprised flight, Red could follow and catch his dinner, thanks to the zigzag lessons he'd learned.

Sometimes he picked up small snacks of fat crickets and other insects. Ground-nesting birds were always a good find. The young birds as well as the eggs made a tasty mid-day snack. Red quickly learned that the best times for good hunting were just after dawn and just before dusk, so he often snoozed during the day.

Fall came, and small creatures grew fatter in preparation for their winter hibernation. Red's meals became larger. He found he could store extra food by digging a cache, or hole, with his feet; then he would tamp the dirt firmly over his cache with his nose.

He began to look for sheltered places to sleep. Hollow logs, openings under rocks, small caves, or even a thick bush with branches low to the ground made safe napping places. Red was always careful. Although he was a predator,

there were other predators only too happy to make a meal of *him.* Bobcats, eagles, coyotes, and even wolves, could be a threat.

When the winter snow came, Red kept warm by curling himself in a circle and wrapping his bushy tail over his nose, eyes, head, and part of his back. As he slept his breath circulated through the hairs on his tail and provided warmth.

About this time Red found a female fox, a vixen, and they began to hunt together. Hunting in snow was not

18

Fox tracks, resembling a dotted line, glisten in the new-fallen snow.

quite so easy as in summer and fall. Their keen hearing and sense of smell told them where mice were hiding beneath the snow. They would sniff out the small creatures, dig them up, and leap high in the air to come down with both front feet securely pinning their prey. Sometimes they used their long noses to "snowplow" after their meal.

During their winter hunting they also searched for a den in which to raise a family later. There were many possible choices. An abandoned badger or woodchuck den might be just the thing. A dry cave under rocks or a big log would do, but a den on the sunny side of a hill overlooking a meadow or valley would be best.

Red and his mate hunted well enough to survive the long winter. And they were clever enough to escape the predators who tried to catch them. When spring arrived, life became easier.

Red, the young hunter, was now a successful adult fox, ready for lots of new adventures.

by Robert Brownridge

A thick white blanket of snow had fallen during the night. All the animals of Deep Green Wood were met by the dazzling sight as they stuck their heads out of their dens.

"Whoopee!" yelled Sammy Squirrel. He ran down his tree and jumped head-first into a soft, fluffy snowdrift.

Soon the woods were alive with small animals playing in the snow.

"Hi, Rangers," called Ranger Rick, who had just appeared. His air of gloom did not match his cheery words.

"Hi, Ranger Rick," said Sammy. "You don't look very happy."

"I've been talking with Ranger Tom and he told me to be on the lookout for snowmobiles," said Ranger Rick.

"What's a snowmobile?" asked Morgan Mockingbird, swooping down nearby.

"It's like a small car with skis on it instead of wheels," explained Rick. "It goes through snow where a car would get stuck. It can even leave the trails and drive almost anywhere."

"They won't run over our homes, will they?" asked Margie Meadow Mouse.

"I'm afraid that at the speed they'll be going they won't even see your house, Margie," said Rick. "I hope you'll be able to see them in time to get out of their way."

"Hey, Rick, I hear something funny," said Snowshoe Hare as he tilted his ears toward the big field beyond the woods. Everyone turned and listened.

"That's a snowmobile," growled Rick grimly. The noisy snowmobile plowed in

4 Reddy Fox Gets Chased!

view, kicking up a big cloud of snow behind it.

"What's that running in front of it?" asked Margie Meadow Mouse.

"That's Reddy Fox," called Morgan Mockingbird from his perch up in a tree. "Why are they chasing him?"

"Just for the fun of it," said Rick sadly. "Ranger Tom told me they chase an animal until it drops from exhaustion. Then they go away. The hot, exhausted animal lies in the cold snow and catches pneumonia. It may even die and the people wouldn't know it."

"Hey, Rick," interrupted Davey Deer. "It looks like Reddy Fox is in real trouble. He can't get away from that snowmobile!"

"You're right," answered Ranger Rick. "We should help him out, even if he is a predator."

"But why?" Snowshoe Hare inquired crossly. "Reddy Fox chases *me* every chance he gets. Last time he almost caught me."

"You can run and hide from predators," said Rick. "They usually catch only the old, the weak, or the careless, but they keep wildlife in balance. Too many animals and too little food means more trouble for everybody. We could all be wiped out by hunger and disease. Reddy keeps us all on our toes."

"We'd better do something quickly," cried Morgan Mockingbird from his lookout on a tree branch. "Reddy is fading fast!"

Suddenly Rick saw a way. His voice crackled with excitement as he shouted his orders. "Sammy, Chester Chipmunk, and all you tree climbers!" he called.

"Get up in that big snow-covered fir tree on the edge of the clearing. Snowshoe Hare, you race over and lead

Reddy under that tree. When I give the signal, push the snow off the branches.''

Snowshoe Hare raced off to catch up with the fox. ''Hey, Reddy, follow me,'' he called when his old enemy got close.

The tired fox turned once again and followed the hare. As the two animals ran under the tree, Ranger Rick yelled, ''Now! Push hard!''

All the animals up in the tree pushed hard on the snow-covered branches. A huge blanket of snow fell earthward.

''Bombs away!'' screeched Morgan.

The rapidly moving snowmobile suddenly disappeared in the cloud of snow. The motor sputtered, coughed, and died.

''Bull's-eye!'' This was the happy voice of Ranger Tom, who had arrived at the height of the excitement.

''Hi, Ranger Tom,'' called Rick. ''What brings you out here today?''

''I had heard about some snow-mobilers chasing animals,'' replied Tom, ''so I came out to stop them. But I see I'm not needed.''

''They sure did a fine job,'' added a happy but exhausted Reddy Fox.

''That's the first time I ever followed a hare to save myself. I usually have something else in mind.''

''I know,'' added the wary hare, ''and I've never asked a fox to chase me, either!''

''That's fine,'' laughed Ranger Tom. ''Shows you how trouble can bring us all together.'' He went over to the snowmobile.

''What happened?'' gasped the driver.

''Let's say it was Nature taking its course,'' replied Ranger Tom. ''You were trying to run that poor fox to death.''

''I was just playing a little game of tag,'' protested the driver.

''Tag!'' laughed Tom grimly. ''You just like to run the animals until they're too tired to move. And then you let them freeze to death. You're not only causing suffering, but you're disturbing wildlife and destroying their homes and habitat,

too. When you use a machine like that, stay on the trails marked for visitors!''

"All right," answered the driver. "I really didn't think I was doing any harm, but maybe I'd better get back to the trail."

"You sure told him off," laughed Ollie when the snowmobile had chugged away.

"Ranger Tom," said Rick, "I wish we could make everyone realize that every kind of animal plays an important part in nature. When they are eliminated by people who haven't carefully studied nature's plan, there's always trouble—lots of it."

"And we don't need any more of that," called out Wise Old Owl.

"On your way, everybody," called Rick, "before Reddy recovers and realizes how hungry he is and how good we look!"

With that warning, all the animals scattered and returned to playing, hiding, and hunting in the snow.

5 Some Other Foxes

THE GRAY FOX

Have you ever seen a fox that climbs trees? The gray fox does! He also tree-sits and leaps from tree to tree. Because he likes dense underbrush he is also called the "wood fox."

He has a long, bushy tail tipped with black and with a long dark stripe down the top. His fur is gray flecked—salt and pepper—but his undercoat is buff. He is a very good hunter.

ARCTIC FOX and KIT FOX

In winter the arctic fox is almost invisible, his white fur blending into the arctic world. In summer his fur matches the dull brown color of the summer tundra. During the cold polar winter he wanders widely, following the polar bear and picking up seal scraps. In summer he hunts for ground squirrels and mice and stores extra food for the winter.

The kit fox, smallest of the North American foxes, has extremely large, pointed ears. He can move each ear, one-at-a-time, and listen in two directions at once. He can even hear a desert rat scampering across sand. This desert fox is the fastest runner of all foxes, a dazzling zigzagger. Wearing a buff-yellow coat, he blends easily into his desert background.

Does the arctic fox at left look white to you? In some regions the "white" coats are blue. To keep warm, the arctic fox has furred feet and short rounded ears. Bigger ones would freeze.

All curled up, one of the kit foxes at right sneaks a peek. Snoozing during the hot desert day, kit foxes hunt at night when it is cooler.

26

FENNEC and BAT-EARED FOX

Extreme desert heat makes a night hunter of the African fennec. His pale sand color is perfect for his home in the deserts of northern Africa and the Sinai and Arabian peninsulas. His strong front legs dig a hole in the desert sand so rapidly that he seems to "sink into the ground." His legs kick so fast that it's difficult to see their movements.

He lives on small rodents, birds and their eggs, insects and lizards. Dates are a special treat.

The fennec is the smallest fox of all; from the tip of his nose to end of his tail is only eighteen inches.

Just like your parents, the bat-eared fox whistles to call his young.

This friendly, curious fox lives in the dry areas of eastern and southern Africa. His coat is yellowish brown with a dark streak running across the eyes and down the center of the nose. He has long ears—almost five inches long—which flatten against his head like those of a cat when he is alarmed.

Pups are born in a den almost any time from December to April. They quickly learn from their parents to find and eat insects, rodents, birds, or eggs and fruits. But their favorite food is termites!

Left: **With his four-inch-long ears, the tiny fennec of North Africa listens for prey.**

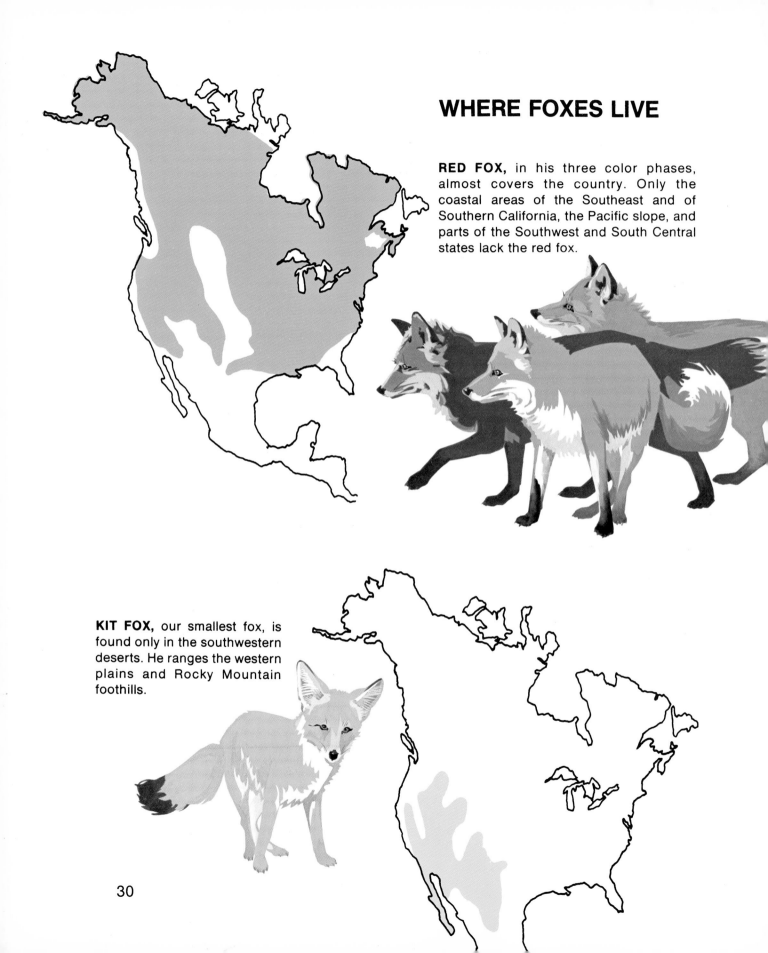

WHERE FOXES LIVE

RED FOX, in his three color phases, almost covers the country. Only the coastal areas of the Southeast and of Southern California, the Pacific slope, and parts of the Southwest and South Central states lack the red fox.

KIT FOX, our smallest fox, is found only in the southwestern deserts. He ranges the western plains and Rocky Mountain foothills.

30

GRAY FOX favors rough, hilly country or heavy woods. Range: Southern swamps to northern forests, southwestern deserts, Pacific Coastal Area, and into Mexico.

ARCTIC FOX, both blue and white phases, lives in the far North and roams the Arctic region, mostly near the shore.

31

WHEN YOU SEE A FOX . . .

Admire his full beautiful coat of golden red fur and his bushy tail tipped with white. All red foxes are not actually red; some are black with white-tipped hairs, others reddish brown or yellowish. But the red fox always has a white-tipped tail. He uses this tail to keep his balance as he hunts, and in winter as a blanket to cover his black nose and feet.

Notice the way he moves. Trotting gracefully along his way, he leaves dainty tracks showing four claws and small pads. The hind tracks fit perfectly into the front tracks. Long legged, with strong back muscles, and built more like a race horse than a dog, a fox can easily outrun foxhounds.

Look for the red fox in open country, along paths and trails, on wood roads, at the edges of woods and fields. He knows the location of gates and holes in fences, and crosses streams on fallen trees or stepping stones. Although the fox usually hunts at night, he is often abroad during the day. Watch and you may see him swinging along a path, an intelligent, clever, and cunning animal.

CREDITS

Les Blacklock red fox cover; Steven C. Wilson pages 2-3; Dave Mech 8, 9, 11 bottom; Leonard Lee Rue III 11 top, 14 top, 24-25; Wilford Miller 12, 13, 16, 17, 18 -19, 26; Maurice C. Hornocker 14-15; Gabe Cherem 19; Chuck McAbery 27; George H. Harrison 28; Christina Locke, Photo Researchers, Inc. 29; Olive Glasgow 32; F. Eugene Hester back cover. Drawings by Frank Fretz 30-31.

NATIONAL WILDLIFE FEDERATION

Thomas L. Kimball	*Executive Vice President*
J. A. Brownridge	*Administrative Vice President*
James D. Davis	*Book Development*

Staff for This Book

EDITOR	Russell Bourne
ASSOCIATE EDITOR	Bonnie S. Lawrence
ART DIRECTOR	Donna M. Sterman
ART ASSISTANT	Ellen Robling
RANGER RICK ADVENTURES	J. A. Brownridge
	Robert Brownridge
RANGER RICK ART	Lorin Thompson
COPY EDITOR	Virginia R. Rapport
PRODUCTION AND PRINTING	Jim DeCrevel
	Mel M. Baughman, Jr.
CONSULTANT	Edwin Gould, Ph.D.
	The Johns Hopkins University

OUR OBJECTIVES

To encourage the intelligent management of the life-sustaining resources of the earth—its productive soil, its essential water sources, its protective forests and plantlife, and its dependent wildlife—and to promote and encourage the knowledge and appreciation of these resources, their interrelationship and wise use, without which there can be little hope for a continuing abundant life.